Twenty to Make
Micro Macramé
Jewellery

Suzen Millodot

Search Press

First published in Great Britain 2009
Search Press Limited
Wellwood, North Farm Road,
Tunbridge Wells, Kent TN2 3DR

Reprinted 2010, 2011, 2012

Text copyright © Suzen Millodot 2009

Photographs by Debbie Patterson at
Search Press Studios

Photographs and design copyright
© Search Press Ltd 2009

Print ISBN: 978-1-84448-349-5
Epub ISBN: 978-1-78126-011-1
Mobi ISBN: 978-1-78126-066-1
PDF ISBN: 978-1-78126-120-0

Suppliers
If you have difficulty in obtaining any of the
materials and equipment mentioned in this book,
then please visit the Search Press website for
details of suppliers: www.searchpress.com

Printed in Malaysia

Dedication
For my husband Michel with grateful
thanks for his constant support and
encouragement, not forgetting all the
delicious meals he prepared
along the way!

Contents

Introduction

Macramé is a craft where knowing a little lets you create a lot. A macramé knot is not an isolated knot, it is basically the inter-knotting of a few cords to make an imaginative weave, and you can make marvellous jewellery with only one simple knot repeated many times over. By varying the way that you position the knots, and using two or three coloured cords, you can achieve a wide variety of designs. In this book, we show you the patterns for two very easy knots, the square knot and the lark's head knot, and how to tie them in different ways with only four cords and combine them with beads to make very stylish necklaces and bracelets.

In the 21st century, macramé has grown up: using delicate, colourful cords and lovely beads, it has once again become fashionable as micro macramé.

It will probably not be possible for you to find exactly the same beads and cords that I have used. Don't worry about it, you will find something equally attractive and will enjoy the creativity of making your own designs!

The basic tools shown on the right are needed for all the projects. For most of the projects, nylon micro macramé thread or any beading cord, even waxed cord, can be used. All of these are easily available in bead shops or by mail order.

Basic tools:

Cork place-mat and dressmaker's pins

Sharp scissors

Clear nail polish

Thread zapper (to cut and seal synthetic cords but not silk, wool, cotton or rayon)

Instant glue gel

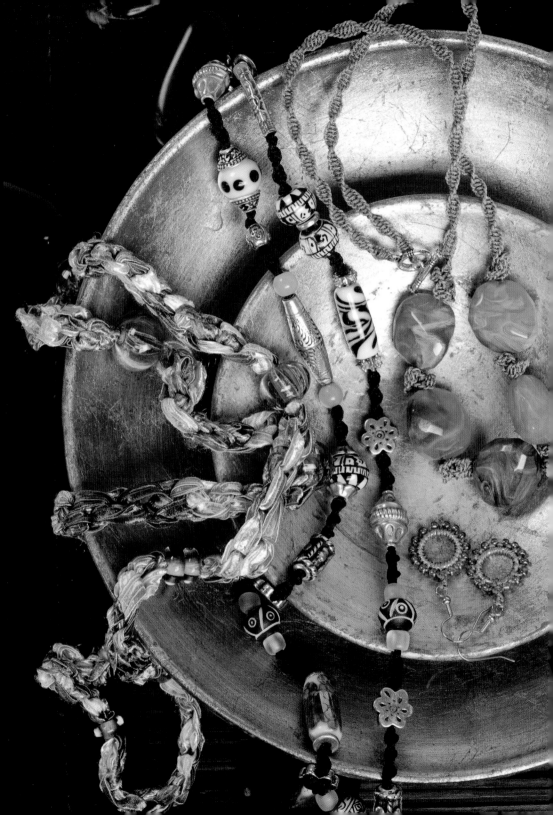

Knots

Lark's head knot

This can be tied horizontally or vertically.

Horizontal version

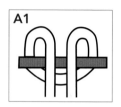 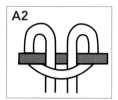 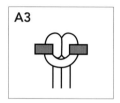 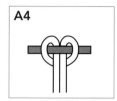

1 Fold the cord in half and place it over the holding cord.

2 Pull the loop down behind the holding cord and pull the two ends down and through the loop.

3 Pull tight.

The reverse side of the lark's head knot.

How to tie vertically to make braids

Alternating lark's head braids

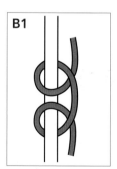 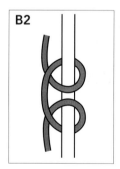 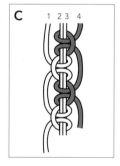 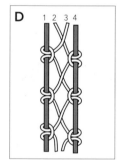

Left direction.

Right direction.

Variation 1.

Variation 2.

Square knot

The square knot is one of the basic macramé knots. Many different patterns can be achieved with this single knot. The following variations are used in some of the jewellery in this book.

First half knot

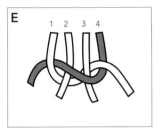

Second half knot to make square knot

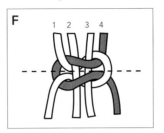

Series of three square knots

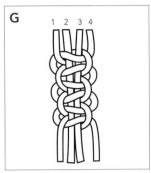

For a right-hand half knot, take cord 4 over 3 and 2 and under cord 1. Take cord 1 under 2 and 3 and up through the loop. Pull tight. A series of these half knots forms a spiral knot (see below).

For a right-hand square knot, once you have tied the right-hand half knot, take cord 4 over 2 and 3 and under 1. Then take cord 1 under 3 and 2 and up through the loop. Pull tight.

The effect achieved by tying a series of square knots.

Spiral knot

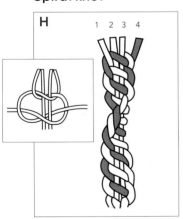

Crossover square knot

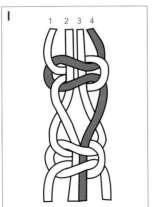

Alternating square knot

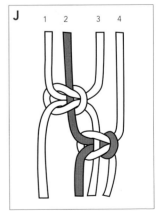

A series of half knots (see diagram E and inset) form a spiral.

Spiral knot variation 1, the crossover square knot, achieved by interchanging knotters and lazy cords.

Spiral knot variation 2, the alternating square knot, in which knots are tied on alternate cords.

Lampwork Necklace

Materials:

Blue nylon micro macramé thread, 2
    pieces: 1 metre (39¼in) and
    4 metres (157½in)

Hook and eye closure

7 lampwork glass beads with
    large holes

Finished length:

48cm (19in), including closures

Knots used:

Square (see diagram)

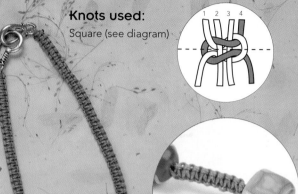

Instructions:

1 'Uncurl' the macramé thread by
wetting it and letting it dry straight
– it dries in minutes. Prepare the ends
with clear nail polish to stiffen them for
threading.

2 Thread both cords halfway through the
eye of the closure, so that the closure sits
in the centre of each. Pin the work to the
cork mat.

3 Start to make square knots, using the
longer cords to knot around the shorter 'lazy' cords,
which will not be knotted.

4 When your knotting has reached 12cm (4¾in), thread
a bead on to all four cords.

5 Knot another 2.5cm (1in) of square knots.

6 Add another bead.

7 Continue in this way, adding a larger bead in the
centre (the fourth bead).

8 When you have added 7 beads, knot another 11cm (4¼in).

9 Thread the other half of the closure on to the centre (lazy) cords, 12mm
(½in) away from the end of the knotting. Fold the lazy cords back on
themselves and glue down for 12mm (½in). Cut off the excess with the
thread zapper. See the diagram on the right.

10 Now you have the centre lazy cords secured with glue, continue using
the knotting cords to make square knots for the last 12mm (½in) until you
reach the closure.

11 Cut off the excess cord (see diagram, right) with the thread zapper
and put a spot of instant glue gel on the cut ends to secure them.

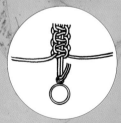

Making a neat finish.

Ethnic Treasure

This version uses the same square knotting technique but with black beading cord and black and ivory coloured beads.

China Blue Necklace

Materials:

Navy blue micro macramé thread,
   2 pieces: 1m (39¼in) and
   4 metres (157½in)

Toggle fastener

9 porcelain Chinese beads with
   large holes

4 small blue beads

Knots used:

Spiral (see right and diagram
H, page 7)

Finished length:

49cm (19in) including
closures

Instructions:

1 Prepare the cords as for the
Lampwork Necklace (page 8).

2 Thread both cords halfway
through the eye of the closure, so
that the closure sits in the centre
of each. Pin the work to the
cork mat.

3 Start to make spiral knots, using
the longer cords to knot around
the shorter 'lazy' cords, which will
not be knotted.

4 When your knotting has
reached 13cm (5in), thread a
large bead on to all four cords.

5 Knot another 2.5cm (1in) of spiral knots.

6 Add a large bead, then a small bead, then
another large bead.

7 Knot another 2.5cm (1in) of spiral knots.

8 Add a large bead, a small bead, a large bead, a small bead and another large bead.

9 Knot another 2.5cm (1in) of spiral knots.

10 Add a large bead, then a small bead, then another large bead.

11 Make another 12cm (4¾in) of spiral knots.

12 Thread the other half of the closure on to the centre (lazy) cords, 12mm (½in) away from
the end of the knotting. Fold the lazy cords back on themselves and glue down for 12mm
(½in). Cut off the excess with the thread zapper (see the diagram at the bottom of page 8).

13 Now you have the centre lazy cords secured with glue, continue using the knotting
cords to make spiral knots for the last 12mm (½in) until you reach the closure.

14 Cut off the excess cord with the zapper, put a spot of instant glue gel on the cut ends
to secure them.

A Passion for Purple

This version, with dark purple micro macramé thread and large purple felt beads has a finished length of 57cm (22½in). You need cords of 130cm (51in) and 500cm (197in) to make it.

Dichroic Glass Pendant

Materials:

Royal blue nylon satin 1mm cord,
   2 pieces: 1 metre (39¼in) and 4 metres (157½in)

Toggle fastener

Dichroic glass pendant

Knots used:

Square (see right, top) and spiral (see right, bottom and H, page 7)

Finished length:

45cm (17¾in) including closures

Instructions:

1 Prepare the cord ends with clear nail polish.

2 Thread both cords halfway through the eye of the closure, so that the closure sits in the centre of each. Pin the work to the cork mat.

3 Start to make square knots, using the longer cords to knot around the shorter 'lazy' cords, which will not be knotted.

4 When your knotting has reached 12cm (4¾in), change to spiral knots for the next 20cm (8in).

5 Resume square knotting for the next 11cm (4¼in). Add the pendant.

6 Thread the other half of the closure on to the centre (lazy) cords, 12mm (½in) away from the end of the knotting. Fold the lazy cords back on themselves and glue down for 12mm (½in). Cut off the excess with the thread zapper (see the diagram at the bottom of page 8).

7 Now you have the centre lazy cords secured with glue, continue using the knotting cords to make square knots for the last 12mm (½in) until you reach the closure.

8 Cut off the excess cord with the zapper and put a spot of instant glue gel on the cut ends to secure them.

Coconut Creation

Spiral and square knots with black 1mm cotton cord combine with a coconut shell pendant and six etched bone beads to create a beautiful, ethnic-looking necklace. Four pieces of cord are needed, two of 1 metre (39¼in) each and two of 4 metres (157½in) each. The knotting is started in the centre (so that the knotting cords will be shorter and easier to manage). The pendant is added to the centre of the two longer pieces of cord with a

horizontal lark's head knot, and the two shorter pieces are threaded in the centre through the loop of the knot to become the lazy cords. There are now four cords on each side. The beads are added to the knotting when required by threading all four cords through each bead then continuing the knotting. When long enough, the two lazy cords on each side are overlapped and glued, and the knotting is continued over them, making the join practically invisible.

Fuchsia Tassel Earrings

Materials:

Fuchsia nylon micro macramé thread,
4 pieces: 36cm (14in) each

2 silver earring hooks

2 Celtic star beads

6 No. 6 seed beads

Approx. 160 small seed beads for tassels

Knots used:

Spiral (see right and diagram H,
page 7) and overhand (see below)

Finished length:

9.5cm (3¾in), but you
can vary this

Instructions:

1 Uncurl the cord by wetting then drying it
straight. Brush clear nail polish on the cord ends.

2 Thread two pieces of cord through the loop on
the earring hook, placing it in the centre of the cords,
then fold them in half.

3 Thread a no. 6 seed bead on to the four ends of the
cords, moving it up to just below the earring hook.

4 Thread on the star bead and another no. 6 seed
bead. Pin the work to the cork mat.

5 Make ten spiral knots (or more if you would like a longer earring).

6 Add another no. 6 seed bead.

7 On each of the four cords, thread seventeen to twenty small
seed beads (make each one a different length) to make a tassel.

8 At the end of each cord, make a small overhand knot (see right,
top diagram) as close to the last bead as possible. If an overhand
knot is too small and goes through the bead hole, you can make a
double overhand knot (see right, bottom).

9 Cut off the excess cords with the thread zapper. Seal with a tiny
drop of instant glue gel.

10 Repeat from step 1 to make a matching earring.

An overhand knot.

*A double overhand knot,
useful if a single knot goes
through the bead hole.*

Chinese Charm

Use blue nylon micro macramé thread, Chinese porcelain beads and
blue seed beads to create these lovely oriental earrings.

Two-Tone Spiral Necklace

Materials:

Blue nylon micro macramé thread, 2 pieces: 2 metres (78in) each

Purple nylon micro macramé thread, 2 pieces: 2 metres (78in) each

7 lampwork glass beads

Toggle fastener

Knots used:

Spiral (see right and diagram H, page 7). Knot from the centre outwards in order to work with shorter knotting cords. By alternating knotting and lazy cords after each bead, you change the visible outer colour.

Finished length:

47cm (18½in) including closures

Instructions:

1 Prepare the cord by uncurling it, as in previous projects. Brush clear nail polish on the ends.

2 Thread all four cords through the largest bead, placing it at the centre of the cords. Pin the work to the cork mat.

3 Make 4.5cm (1¾in) of spiral knots.

4 Add a bead.

5 Change the knotting and 'lazy' cords and make another 4.5cm (2in) of spiral knots. The knotting will now be in the second colour.

6 Add a bead. Change the knotting and 'lazy' cords and repeat steps 3, 4 and 5 until you have three beads (as well as the centre bead).

7 Thread the loop half of the closure on to the centre (lazy) cords, 12mm (½in) away from the end of the knotting. Fold the lazy cords back on themselves and glue down for 12mm (½in). Cut off the excess with the thread zapper (see the diagram at the bottom of page 8).

8 Now you have the centre lazy cords secured with glue, continue using the knotting cords to make spiral knots for the last 12mm (½in) until you reach the closure.

9 Cut off the excess cord with the zapper and put a spot of instant glue gel on the cut ends to secure them.

10 Repeat steps 3 to 9 with the cords on the other side of the centre bead, to finish the necklace.

16

Beautiful Bone

This version is made using turquoise and grey micro macramé thread with Chinese etched bone beads and a spiral knot tassel, made in the same way as the earrings on page 14.

Shades of Pink Necklace

Materials:

Pink/red novelty knitting yarn,
2 pieces: 1 metre (39¼in)
and 6.4 metres (252in)

5 large beads with large holes

A smaller bead with a very
large hole

Tools:

Basic tools plus a 12cm (4¾in)
piece of fuse wire (to help
thread the yarn through
the beads)

Finished length:

64cm (25¼in)

Knots used:

Square knots, but knotted
around only one lazy cord
(see diagram) as the yarn is
thick. Start in the centre in
order to work with shorter
length knotting cords.

Instructions:

1 Thread the short piece of yarn
through the centre bead until it is
halfway along. This makes the
lazy cord.

2 Cut the long piece into two
pieces. Thread them through the
large bead until the bead is in the
centre of both pieces.

3 Secure the yarn next to the bead with a pin, on the side that will not be knotted yet, to
prevent slipping. Pin to the cork mat.

4 With the short piece of yarn in the middle (lazy cord), make square knots with the two longer
pieces. Make 8cm (3¼in) of knotting.

5 Add a large bead.

6 Knot another 8cm (3¼in) of square knotting.

7 Add another large bead.

8 Continue knotting for approx. 15cm (6in) or as long as you wish. Unpin from the cork mat.

9 Turn the work around, remove the anchor pin next to the centre bead. Repin to the cork mat.

10 Repeat steps 4 to 8 on the other side.

11 Thread the right-hand side of the square knotting through the smaller bead from right to left.

12 Thread the left-hand side of the square knotting through the smaller bead from left to right.

13 If the yarn is synthetic, cut and seal the excess yarn with the zapper on each side of the small bead to make a neat finish.

14 If necessary, put a small dot of instant glue gel inside the finishing bead, to prevent the yarn slipping out.

Green Earth

Use green, blue and earth shade cords of 1.2 metres (47¼in) and 8 metres (314in) for this necklace of 96cm (37¾in).

Moonstone Necklace

Materials:

Black 0.8mm beading cord, 4 pieces,
  2 of 1metre (39¼in) each and 2 of 1.5 metres
  (58in) each

Toggle fastener

2 decorative spacers (optional)

10 filigree bead caps (optional)

32 to 38 medium sized beads, various shapes
  in black, white, moonstone, pearl and crystal

48 to 56 small, mostly round, beads in assorted
  black, white, pearl and crystal

Knots used:

Square (see diagram)
and overhand (see
page 14, bottom)

Finished length:

45cm (17¾in) including closures

Instructions:

1 Start in the centre of the first cord,
thread on a large bead and make an
overhand knot (see page 14, bottom) on
each side of the bead.

2 2cm (¾in) away, make another
overhand knot, add a different bead and
make another overhand knot to secure it.

3 2cm (¾in) away, make another overhand knot,
add a small bead, a larger bead then another small bead, and make an overhand knot.

4 Add another medium-sized bead, (with the optional bead caps if used).

5 Turn the work around and repeat steps 2 to 4, using slightly different beads.

6 Continue until the knotted and beaded section is 29cm (11½in) long. Set aside.

7 On the second cord, repeat steps 1 to 5 until the beaded section is 30cm (11¾in) long.
Set aside.

8 On the third cord, repeat steps 1 to 5 until the beaded section is 31cm (12¼in) long.
Set aside.

9 On the fourth cord, repeat steps 1 to 5 until the beaded section is 32cm (12½in) long.

10 Gather the four cords together in a pleasing combination (if you need to, you can move any
bead slightly to the left or right by moving the knots). Add a bead spacer at each end of the

knotting (or if not using bead spacers, make an overhand knot with all four cords, as shown in the design below). Pin the work to the cork mat at the junction of all four cords.

11 On one side, make 6cm (2³⁄₈in) of square knotting using the longer cords as the knotting cords. Add the toggle fastener and make a neat finish in the same way as in steps 9 to 11 on page 8.

12 Finish the other side in the same way as in step 11.

Coral Gold

Use Celtic pewter beads with red glass and coral beads and orange and gold seed beads to make this gorgeous necklace.

Chinese Rings

Materials:

1mm Chinese knotting
   cord, 1 piece: 96cm
   (37¾in) long

Flat, fused glass bead
   with large hole

Knots used:

Square (see diagram)

Instructions:

1 Stiffen cord ends with clear nail polish.

2 Fold the piece of cord in half and thread it through the bead.

3 Arrange it so that it goes around your finger (or the future wearer's finger) once, slightly loose, with an overlap of 5mm (¼in).

4 Put a couple of spots of instant glue gel on the overlapping join to secure it. Pull it backwards through the bead so that the join is inside the hole and does not show. Pin the work to the cork mat.

5 With the remaining long ends of the cord, make square knots around the fixed ring of cords. Make sure the knots are tightly woven and as close together as possible, to make the ring fairly stiff.

6 To finish, cut the free ends of the knotting and seal them with the thread zapper as close to the knotting as possible.

7 Put a spot of instant glue gel on each end to secure them.

Heavenly Blue

Choose cord colours to bring out the beauty of your bead. This bright blue looks striking with the iridescent sheen in the bead.

Scalloped Bracelet

Materials:

Purple 1mm satin cord, 2 pieces:
  50cm (19¾in) and 180cm (70¾in)

Approx. 108 no. 6 seed beads

Toggle fastener

Finished length:

22cm (8¾in)

Knots used:

Vertical lark's head knots around central lazy cords, alternating left and right sides (see diagram right), and square knots (see diagram far right)

Instructions:

1 Stiffen cord ends with clear nail polish.

2 Thread both cords through the loop end of the toggle until they are both centrally placed at the toggle.

3 Fold them down and pin on to the cork mat to start knotting. Make one square knot with the longer cords around the shorter cords.

4 Thread three beads on to the left cord.

5 Make a vertical lark's head knot with the left cord around the two central cords.

6 Thread three beads on to the right cord.

7 Make a vertical lark's head knot with the right cord around the two central cords.

8 Continue adding beads and knotting until you reach 1.25cm (½in) before the length you require.

9 Thread the toggle fastener on to the central cords.

10 Finish in exactly the same way as in the Lampwork Necklace on page 8, by cutting and glueing down the lazy cords and continuing knotting over them, finishing with a square knot.

Beaded Beauty

This alternative uses dark red Chinese knotting cords and coral and gold seed beads for a subtle but sumptuous effect.

Sea-Green Earrings

Materials:

Green nylon micro macramé thread, two pieces: 66cm (26in) each

Two earring hooks

Two turquoise jump rings 12mm (½in) in diameter

28 to 30 seed beads

Knots used:

Vertical lark's head around the ring (right) and spiral (see right, below and diagram H, page 7)

Finished length:

4cm (1½in)

Instructions:

1 Prepare the cords by wetting them then drying them straight to take out the unwanted curl (the thread dries in minutes). Stiffen the ends with clear nail polish.

2 Leave about 12.5cm (5in) of cord free before tying a vertical lark's head knot (see the top diagram) in the right direction towards the centre of the ring.

3 Add a seed bead, then tie another vertical lark's head knot below the first, in the same direction.

4 Repeat step 3, adding a bead before each new knot until you have gone all around the ring and reached the beginning again.

5 Decide how long you wish the spiral knotting to be between the ring and the earring hook, for example I wanted 8mm (¼in), then thread the two cords through the loop of the earring hook, 8mm (¼in) away from the ring. Pin to the cork mat.

6 Fold the free ends over the loop of the earring hook. Cut them 8mm (¼in) and glue them down exactly as in steps 9, 10 and 11 on page 8.

7 Make spiral knots around the centre cord back down to the ring. Cut and seal the ends and secure them with a dot of instant glue gel.

8 Repeat steps 2 to 7 to make the second earring.

Perfect Pink
These earrings were made in the same way but with silver jump rings and seed beads and dark pink micro macramé thread.

Lavender Necklace

Materials:

Lavender Chinese 1mm knotting cord, 2 pieces: 210cm (82¾in) each

Toggle (or hook and eye) closure

Approx. 72 no. 6 seed beads

Finished length:

48cm (19in) including closures

Knots used:

Crossover square knots: interchanging knotting and lazy cords after each knot (see diagram below)

Instructions:

1 Prepare the ends of the cords with clear nail polish.

2 Thread the two cords through the loop of the closure until the halfway point of the cords.

3 Pin to the cork mat to start knotting. Make one square knot.

4 Bring the outside cords into the centre, to become the lazy cords.

5 With the previously lazy cords now on the outside, use them to tie another square knot. The knotting will look lacy.

6 Repeat steps 4 and 5 until the knotting is 6.5cm (2½in) long.

7 Add a bead on to each outside cord before bringing them to the centre to become the lazy cords.

8 Use the cords that are now on the outside to make a square knot, as before.

9 Repeat steps 7 and 8 for another 30cm (11¾in).

10 Resume knotting without beads, as in steps 4 and 5, until another 5.5cm (2¼in) has been knotted.

11 Add the other half of the closure, threading it on to the centre lazy cords.

12 Cut, trim and glue down following steps 9, 10 and 11 on page 8.

Precious Pearls
Black cord and pearl and clear seed beads make this a striking alternative.

Oriental Agate Necklace

Materials:

Black 1.25mm beading cord, 2 pieces: each 210cm (83in) long

Toggle (or hook and eye fastener)

Handmade agate pendant

Jump rings to attach the pendant to the knotted necklace

Finished length:

48cm (18½in) including closures

Tools:

Basic tools, plus two pairs of needle-nosed pliers to attach the pendant to the knotting with jump rings

Knots used:

Crossover square knots: interchanging knotting and lazy cords after each knot (see diagram)

Instructions:

1 Thread the two cords through one half of the closure until it is halfway along the cords.

2 Attach the work to the cork mat and fold the cords down, to start knotting.

3 Make a square knot.

4 Bring the outside cords into the centre, to become the lazy cords.

5 With the previously lazy cords now on the outside, use them to tie another square knot. The knotting will look lacy.

6 Continue in this way until the knotting is 43cm (17in) long.

7 Follow steps 9, 10 and 11 on page 8 to finish the necklace.

8 Add the pendant to the centre of the knotting, using the jump rings. Make sure you open the jump rings by twisting one side towards you and the other side away from you with the pliers, then closing again by reversing this action.

Autumn Flower

Rusty red knotting cord and a brass flower pendant create a very different look.

Pink Satin Necklace

Materials:

Pink 1mm satin cord, 2 pieces:
one 120cm (47in) long and
one 480cm (189in)

1 toggle (or hook and eye)
closure

26 medium sized beads with
large holes

Knots used:

Square (see diagram)

Finished length:

48cm (19in) including closures

Instructions:

1 Prepare the ends of the cords with clear nail polish.

2 Thread the cords through one half of the closure up to the halfway point.

3 Attach the work to the cork mat with pins.

4 Make three square knots, knotting the longer cords around the shorter
(lazy) cords.

5 Add a bead to the centre cords, bringing the longer cords down either side of
the bead.

6 Knot two more square knots.

7 Add a bead to the centre cords, bringing the longer cords down either side of
the bead.

8 Repeat steps 6 and 7, until the knotting is 44cm (17¼in) long.

9 Follow steps 9, 10 and 11 on page 8 to finish the necklace, making three square
knots over the glued centre cords to match the other side.

Crystal Clear

Royal blue satin cord, knotted in exactly the same way, with clear,
multicoloured beads, creates a very different look.

Porcelain Bracelet

Materials:

Blue nylon micro macramé
thread, three pieces: two
120cm (47in) long, the other
60cm (23½in) long

Approx. 15 medium-sized
Chinese porcelain beads
with fairly large holes

4 small beads to finish

Knots used:

Overhand (see page 14)
and square (see below)

Finished length:

24cm (9½in)

Instructions:

1 Uncurl the cords by dampening them, then brush clear nail polish on to
the ends.

2 Take the two longer pieces of cord, leaving 13cm (5in) free on the ends. Make an
overhand knot (see page 14, bottom), then pin to the cork mat.

3 Thread a medium-sized bead on to the two cords.

4 Make another overhand knot as close to the bead as possible (use a large pin to hold
the cord next to the bead as you pull the knot tight).

5 Repeat steps 3 and 4 until the bracelet reaches the desired length (somewhere
between 20 to 23cm (7¾ to 9in) depending on the size of the future wearer's wrist.

6 Pin the bracelet to the cork mat, in a circle, with the ends (after the last knots) going in
opposite directions and overlapping by at least 2cm (¾in).

7 Take the 60cm (23½in) cord, fold it in two and place the centre point behind the
overlapping cords, next to the last overhand knot.

8 Secure it with a pin, then make a series of six square knots around the four cords. The
square knots will make a 'sleeve' around the cords. The square knots must be tight, but
not too tight. They must hold the cords inside firmly but allow movement of the cords to
make the bracelet larger to slip on the wrist, then smaller again once on the wrist.

9 Add a small bead to each of the free ends. Leave approx. 2 to 6cm (¾ to 2¼in) after the square knot sleeve on each side. Make an overhand knot next to each small bead to secure it on to the cord. Trim the excess cord.

10 Add a spot of instant glue gel to each end knot, to prevent it from coming undone.

Bronze Blaze

This version has pink and beige cords and dichroic glass beads with a bronze glow. The beaded ends are also longer than in the project.

Braided Watch Strap

Materials:
1mm turquoise cotton cord, 4 pieces: 2 of 50cm (19¾in) and 2 of 1 metre (39¼in)

Watch

Toggle closure

Knots used:
Square knots (see below) and alternating vertical lark's head knots: the knotting cords are in the centre and the lazy cords are on either side of the knotting

Finished length:
19cm (7½in) including watch and closures

Instructions:
1 Thread the longest cord through the loop of the watch (this will be the knotting cord for the lark's head knots).

2 Fold the cord in two and pin the watch and cords to the cork mat.

3 With the shorter piece, make one square knot around the centre cords.

4 Take the third cord from the left, bring it across and make a vertical lark's head knot on the left-hand outside cord.

5 Take the second cord from the left across and make a vertical lark's head knot on the right-hand outside cord.

6 Repeat this knotting pattern from one side to the other until the knotting is 6.5cm (2½in) long. This length is for a 18cm (7in) wrist. Depending on the wrist size of the future wearer, you may need to make it longer.

7 Thread the loop of the toggle on to the centre cords, about 1cm (³⁄₈in) from the last knot.

8 Follow steps 9, 10 and 11 on page 8 to finish the strap, but use scissors rather than the thread zapper to cut the cotton cords.

9 Repeat steps 1 to 8 to make the strap on the other side of the watch, attaching the other half of the toggle fastener.

Perfect Timing

For this variation, use black 1mm cotton cord. Two horizontal lark's head knots are used to attach the cord to the watch, but otherwise the knotting is the same.

Knotwork Bracelet

Materials:

Asian knotting cord, 2 pieces: each 175cm (69in) long, one purple and one pink

Celtic pewter button, 17mm (¾in) to fasten the bracelet

Finished length:

24cm (9½in) including the loop and button

Knots used:

Square knots tied on alternate cords: cords 1 and 3 around cord 2, then cords 4 and 2 around cord 3 (see diagram)

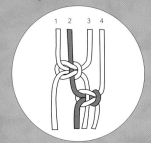

Instructions:

1 Find the centre of the two cords and pin to the cork board.

2 Make a series of vertical lark's head knots for 4.75cm (1¾in), all in the same direction.

3 With the knots towards the outside, make a loop of the lark's head knots. Check that this loop will fit around the button you have chosen for the fastening.

4 Make a square knot with the four cords that result from making the loop, to secure it.

5 When you are satisfied that the loop is the correct size, make a square knot by tying cords 1 and 3 around cord 2.

6 Below this make another square knot by tying cords 4 and 2 around cord 3. Tying all the square knots all in the same direction, i.e. from right to left, exactly as shown in the diagram at the top of this page, makes a firmer braid.

7 When your knotting reaches 19cm (7½in), thread the button on to the two centre cords.

8 Secure the button in exactly the same way as the closure is attached in steps 9 to 11 on page 8.

Apricot Delight

This necklace is made with grey and apricot cords, with a Celtic pewter bead as a centrepiece. You need two 3.5 metre (137¾in) pieces of cord. The finished length is 49cm (19¼in) including the loop and button.

Celtic Necklace

Materials:

1mm turquoise satin cord, 2 pieces:
  200cm (78¾in) and 500cm (196¾in)

8 different pewter Celtic beads

One pewter Celtic pendant

One Celtic button, 17mm (¾in)

Finished length:

52cm (20½in) including
the loop and button

Knots used:

Vertical lark's head knots (see below,
left) and square knots (below, right)

Instructions:

1 Brush clear nail polish on the ends of the cords, to
stiffen them.

2 Find the exact centre of the shortest cord. Find
the point 1 metre (39¼in) from the end of the longest
cord. Pin them both to the cork mat at this point, (one
of the cords will be longer). Make 4.75cm (1¾in) of
vertical lark's head knots all in the same direction, with
the longer cord knotted around the shorter cord.

3 With the knots towards the outside, make a loop of
the lark's head knots. Check that this loop will fit around the
button you have chosen for the fastening.

4 When you are satisfied that the loop is the correct size,
make a square knot with the four cords that result from
making the loop, to secure it. You now have four cord lengths,
three short ones and one long one.

5 Use the longer cord to knot vertical lark's head knots around
the other three cord lengths.

6 Continue making vertical lark's head knots for 15cm (6in), not including the loop.

7 Add a Celtic octagonal bead. Make two more lark's head knots.

8 Add a Celtic star bead. Make two more lark's head knots.

9 Add a Celtic brick bead. Make two more lark's head knots.

10 Add a 12mm (½in) Celtic sphere. Make three more lark's head knots.

11 Add the pewter pendant. Make three more lark's head knots.

12 Add a 12mm (½in) Celtic sphere. Make two more lark's head knots.

13 Repeat step 9.

14 Repeat step 8.

15 Add a Celtic octagonal bead.

16 Continue making the lark's head knots for another 14cm (5½in).

17 Thread the button on to the two centre cords.

18 Do steps 9 to 11 from page 8 to finish the necklace.

Black Beauty

This bracelet is made in the same way except that the beads are grouped in the middle after 5cm (2in) of lark's head knots. The lengths of cord needed are 1 metre (39¼in) and 2.5 metres (98½in). The finished length is 20cm (8in), including the loop and button.

Emerald Green Necklace

Materials:

Emerald green 1.25mm knotting cord,
  2 pieces: 4 metres (157½in) each

39 assorted blue beads

Toggle (or hook and eye) fastener

Knots used:

Square (see diagram below) and
overhand (see page 14, bottom)

Finished length:

69cm (27¼in) including
closures

Instructions:

1 Brush the cord ends with clear nail
polish and let them dry.

2 Thread on one half of the fastener to
the centre point of both cords.

3 Fold the cords down and pin on to the
cork mat.

4 Make four square knots.

5 Add one bead to three of the cords (the
last one stays unbeaded).

6 Make an overhand knot (see page 14) 4cm
(1½in) away from the end of the square knots.

7 Repeat steps 5 and 6.

8 Continue adding beads and making overhand knots until the knotting is
64cm (25¼in) long.

9 Do steps 9 to 11 on page 8 to finish the necklace, except you must leave
2.5cm (1in) at the end to make five square knots, to match the beginning.

Pink Creation

This stunning variation features deep pink cords and a selection of beads in pink, purple and blue.

Willow Green Necklace

Materials:

Green nylon micro macramé thread, one piece 220cm (86½in), the other 8 metres (315in) long

5 large beads with large holes

1 toggle fastener

Finished length:

64cm (25¼in) including the closures

Knots used:

Spiral (see diagram below and H, page 7) and overhand (see page 14). This unusual method involves making a braid with spiral knots, then tying an overhand knot in the knotted braid to make a twisted 'bead'.

Instructions:

1 Prepare the cord ends by brushing them with clear nail polish.

2 Thread the cords through the loop of the toggle fastener, finding the mid-point of each cord.

3 Pin the toggle to the cork mat and fold down the cords.

4 Make spiral knots using the long cords to knot around the shorter cords. Knot until the knotting measures 26cm (10¼in).

5 Tie an overhand knot (see page 14, bottom) with the last 4cm (1½in) of the knotted part. This gives a knot of about 1cm (³⁄₈in) in diameter).

6 Thread a bead up close to the knot. Make another 4cm (1½in) of spiral knots. Make an overhand knot with this section of knotting.

7 Repeat step 6.

8 Keep repeating these steps until five beads have been threaded on to the necklace, finishing with a knotted overhand knot.

9 Make spiral knots for another 21cm (8¼in).

10 Finish the necklace following steps 9 to 11 on page 8.

Forest Treasure

You need two pieces of nylon micro macramé cord, one 1.4 metres (55in) and the other 4 metres (157½in), to make this bracelet, which is 22cm (8¾in) long. Add six green beads and twelve bead caps for a really opulent looking bracelet.

Loop and Tassel Lariat

Materials:

Black nylon micro macramé thread, 2 pieces, 150cm (59in) long and 5 metres (195in) long

16 black, white or silver large beads with large holes

9 white medium-sized beads with large holes

4 bead caps with large holes (optional)

11 small beads

1 long narrow bead (optional)

1 silver loop (I used a triangular loop to thread the end of the lariat through, but a circular one would do)

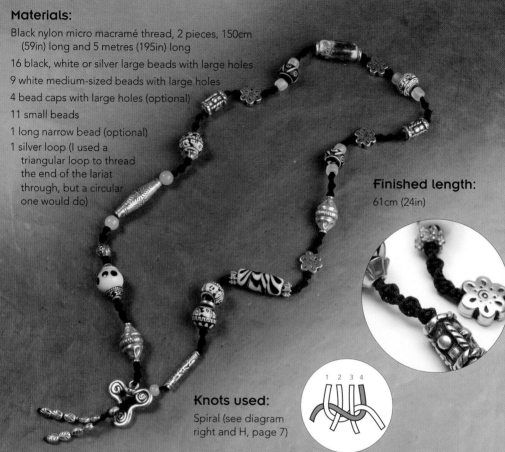

Finished length:

61cm (24in)

Knots used:

Spiral (see diagram right and H, page 7)

Instructions:

1 Wet the micro macramé thread to uncurl it, then brush the ends with clear nail polish.

2 Thread the cords through the loop until it is at the centre point of both cords. Pin to the cork mat and fold down the ends, to start knotting.

3 Make ten spiral knots and add a bead.

4 Make ten spiral knots and add another bead.

5 Continue in this way, varying the sizes and shapes of the beads and slightly varying the lengths of the knotting between the beads, and putting smaller beads either side of some of the larger round ones.

6 Continue until the knotting is 62cm (24½in) long.

7 After this point, the beads must be small enough to pass through the loop.

8 Make 8cm (3¼in) of small beads and spiral knots.

9 Separate the cords and thread small beads on to each cord to make a tassel, one piece 4cm (1½in) long and the other 3.5cm (1¼in) long. Make an overhand knot (see page 14, bottom) at the end of each cord to secure the beads. Add a spot of instant glue gel to make sure they stay knotted.

Lovely Lariat

This lariat is long enough to go round the neck twice: 140cm (55in), and an agate ring was used as the loop to thread the tassel through. Two cords were needed: one of 220cm (86½in) and one of 9 metres (354¼in).

Publisher's Note

If you would like more books on knots
for beaded jewellery, try the following
by the same author:
Chinese Knots for Beaded Jewellery,
Search Press, 2003
Celtic Knots for Beaded Jewellery,
Search Press, 2006 and
*Ornamental Knots for
Beaded Jewellery*,
Search Press, 2008

Acknowledgements

Special thanks to Black Dragon
Crafts in Wales for supplying the
beautiful Celtic beads used in some
of the projects; to Ray Skene of
Celtic Glass in Wales for making
many of the lovely lampwork beads
that feature in this book; to
Sarah Fisher for the gorgeous felt
beads and Marlene Minhas for the
fused glass beads, and to Robin of
www.satincord.com who supplied
the 1mm satin cord and who is
always so knowledgeable and
helpful about everything to do with
cords for knotting.

You are invited to visit the
author's website
www.ornamental-knots.com